SACRE

for Advent and the Christmas Season
2008-2009

SACREDSPACE

for Advent and the Christmas Season
2008-2009

November 30, 2008 to January 4, 2009

from the website www.sacredspace.ie

Jesuit Communication Centre, Ireland

ave maria press AMP notre dame, indiana

Acknowledgment

The publisher would like to thank Alan McGuckian, S.J., Gerry Bourke, S.J., and Piaras Jackson, S.J., for their kind assistance in making this book possible. Correspondence with the Sacred Space team can be directed to feedback@sacredspace.ie. Piaras Jackson, S.J., Gerry Bourke, S.J., Paul Andrews, S.J., and John McDermott welcome all comments on the material or on the site.

Published under license from Michelle Anderson Publishing Pty Ltd., in Australia.

Founded in 1865, Ave Maria Press is a ministry of the Indiana Province of Holy Cross.

www.avemariapress.com

ISBN-10: 1-59471-178-X   ISBN-13: 978-1-59471-178-7

Cover and text design by K. H. Coney.

Printed and bound in the United States of America.

Contents

How to Use This Booklet

We invite you to make a sacred space in your day and spend ten minutes praying here and now, wherever you are, with the help of a prayer guide and scripture chosen specially for each day of Advent and the Christmas Season. Every place is a sacred space so you may wish to have this book in your desk at work or available to be picked up and read at any time of the day, whilst traveling or on your bedside table, a park bench . . . Remember that God is everywhere, all around us, constantly reaching out to us, even in the most unlikely situations. When we know this, and with a bit of practice, we can pray anywhere.

The following pages will guide you through a session of prayer stages.

Something to think and pray about each day this
   week
The Presence of God
Freedom
Consciousness

The Word (leads you to the daily scripture and
   provides help with the text)
Conversation
Conclusion

It is most important to come back to these pages
each day of the week as they are an integral part
of each day's prayer and lead to the scripture and
inspiration points.

Although written in the first person the prayers
are for "doing" rather than for reading out. Each
stage is a kind of exercise or meditation aimed at
helping you to get in touch with God and God's
presence in your life.

We hope that you will join the many people
around the world praying with us in our sacred
space.

The Presence of God

Bless all who worship you, almighty God,
from the rising of the sun to its setting:
from your goodness enrich us,
by your love inspire us,
by your Spirit guide us,
by your power protect us,
in your mercy receive us,
now and always.

November 30–December 6, 2008

Something to think and pray about each day this week:

Reading the Future

Judaism provided the early Church with rich images to describe the final coming of God as the Lord of all history and creation. The gospels drew on that imagery to encourage the early Christians—and us today—to look forward to the day when the Son of Man comes. That day is imminent; be vigilant, watchful in how you live, and confident in your suffering.

For the Christian, the return of Jesus is not a time to be feared; the end is not the end at all but a time of hope, of liberation, of rebirth, of new life. Until that day, Jesus exhorts us to watch and wait, to live a life that stands out from those we live among. "Be on watch and pray always" (Luke 21:36).

The Presence of God
Lord, help me to be fully alive to your holy
presence.
Enfold me in your love.
Let my heart become one with yours.

Freedom
Many countries are at this moment suffering
the agonies of war.
I bow my head in thanksgiving for my freedom.
I pray for all prisoners and captives.

Consciousness
At this moment, Lord, I turn my thoughts to You.
I will leave aside my chores and preoccupations.
I will take rest and refreshment in your presence
Lord.

The Word
The word of God comes down to us through the
scriptures. May the Holy Spirit enlighten my mind
and my heart to respond to the gospel teachings.
(Please turn to your scripture on the following
pages. Inspiration points are there should you
need them. When you are ready, return here to
continue.)

Conversation

Sometimes I wonder what I might say
if I were to meet You in person, Lord.
I might say "Thank You, Lord" for always being
there for me.
I know with certainty there were times when you
carried me.
When through your strength I got through the
dark times in my life.

Conclusion

Glory be to the Father, and to the Son, and to the
Holy Spirit,
As it was in the beginning, is now and ever shall
be,
World without end. Amen

Sunday 30th November,
First Sunday of Advent
Isaiah 63:16b–17, 19, 64:1–8

You, O Lord, are our father; our Redeemer from of old is your name. Why, O Lord, do you make us stray from your ways and harden our heart, so that we do not fear you? Turn back for the sake of your servants, for the sake of the tribes that are your heritage. We have long been like those whom you do not rule, like those not called by your name. O that you would tear open the heavens and come down, so that the mountains would quake at your presence—as when fire kindles brushwood and the fire causes water to boil—to make your name known to your adversaries, so that the nations might tremble at your presence! When you did awesome deeds that we did not expect, you came down, the mountains quaked at your presence. From ages past no one has heard, no ear has perceived, no eye has seen any God besides you, who works for those who wait for him. You meet those who gladly do right, those who remember you in your ways. But you were angry, and we sinned; because you hid yourself we transgressed. We have all become like one who is unclean, and all our righteous deeds are like a filthy cloth. We all fade like a leaf, and our iniquities, like the wind, take us away. There is no one who calls on your name, or attempts to take hold of you; for you have hidden your face from us, and have delivered us into the hand of our iniquity. et, O Lord, you are our Father; we are the clay, and you are our potter; we are all the work of your hand.

- There are a lot of mixed emotions expressed in this passage, and strong ones: repentance, regret, yearning, pleading. Do any of them express something of what I am feeling now?

- Most of all, this passage is asking God to make his presence known.

- God is present here now, and listening to me. What do I want to say?

Monday 1st December   Matthew 8:5–11

When Jesus entered Capernaum, a centurion came to him, appealing to him and saying, "Lord, my servant is lying at home paralyzed, in terrible distress." And he said to him, "I will come and cure him." The centurion answered, "Lord, I am not worthy to have you come under my roof; but only speak the word, and my servant will be healed. For I also am a man under authority, with soldiers under me; and I say to one, 'Go,' and he goes, and to another, 'Come,' and he comes, and to my slave, 'Do this,' and the slave does it." When Jesus heard him, he was amazed and said to those who followed him, "Truly I tell you, in no one in Israel have I found such faith. I tell you, many will come from east and west and will eat with Abraham and Isaac and Jacob in the kingdom of heaven."

- The centurion made an extraordinary leap from his own culture, position, and pride to recognize Jesus' power. Jesus was amazed at his faith.

- Have I the insight to perceive holiness and God's hand at work around me, or am I imprisoned in the stereotypes of my culture?

Tuesday 2nd December Luke 10:21–24

At that same hour Jesus rejoiced in the Holy Spirit and said, "I thank you, Father, Lord of heaven and earth, because you have hidden these things from the wise and the intelligent and have revealed them to infants; yes, Father, for such was your gracious will. All things have been handed over to me by my Father; and no one knows who the Son is except the Father, or who the Father is except the Son and anyone to whom the Son chooses to reveal him." Then turning to the disciples, Jesus said to them privately, "Blessed are the eyes that see what you see! For I tell you that many prophets and kings desired to see what you see, but did not see it, and to hear what you hear, but did not hear it."

- Jesus' mission flows entirely out of his relationship with the Father, and the same God-centered relationship is open to each of us. This is an immense, awe-inspiring privilege.

- Lord, may this knowledge sustain me when I falter, when the journey becomes difficult and I turn my face from you.

Wednesday 3rd December   Isaiah 25:6–10a

O n this mountain the Lord of hosts will make for all peoples a feast of rich food, a feast of well-matured wines, of rich food filled with marrow, of well-matured wines strained clear. And he will destroy on this mountain the shroud that is cast over all peoples, the sheet that is spread over all nations; he will swallow up death for ever. Then the Lord God will wipe away the tears from all faces, and the disgrace of his people he will take away from all the earth, for the Lord has spoken. It will be said on that day, Lo, this is our God; we have waited for him, so that he might save us. This is the Lord for whom we have waited; let us be glad and rejoice in his salvation. For the hand of the Lord will rest on this mountain.

- Do I dare to hope for a great and glorious day in the future when all my tears will be wiped away, when all my shortcomings and failings will count for nothing and I will rest, joyful, in God's loving presence?

- How does the Lord's promise resonate with me? Does it excite me and confirm my deepest hopes? Does it seem to go against the grain of my experience and leave me confused and unsure?

- Can I bring what is in my heart to the Lord in this time of prayer?

Thursday 4th December   Matthew 7:21, 24–27

Jesus said to his disciples, "Not everyone who says to me, 'Lord, Lord,' will enter the kingdom of heaven, but only the one who does the will of my Father in heaven." 'Everyone then who hears these words of mine and acts on them will be like a wise man who built his house on rock. The rain fell, the floods came, and the winds blew and beat on that house, but it did not fall, because it had been founded on rock. And everyone who hears these words of mine and does not act on them will be like a foolish man who built his house on sand. The rain fell, and the floods came, and the winds blew and beat against that house, and it fell—and great was its fall!'

- Lord—there I go again, calling you Lord—look at my life and my actions, not my speeches.

- I do not expect to be judged on pious words, but on the love and justice evident in my life.

Friday 5th December   Matthew 9:27–31

As Jesus went on his way, two blind men followed him, crying loudly, "Have mercy on us, Son of David!" When he entered the house, the blind men came to him; and Jesus said to them, "Do you believe that I am able to do this?" They said to him, "Yes, Lord." Then he touched their eyes and said, "According to your faith let it be done to you." And their eyes were opened.

- From among the crowd the blind men shout out to Jesus using a formal title, Son of David, as though he was a powerful messianic figure dispensing health to crowds. But Jesus waits until he can meet these men in person, in the quiet of the house where he can test and reveal their faith.

- Lord, you do not meet me as one among many, but face to face, on my own, where you can test the truth of my words, free from the illusions of mass emotion.

Saturday 6th December   Isaiah 30:19–21, 23–26

Truly, O people in Zion, inhabitants of Jerusalem, you shall weep no more. He will surely be gracious to you at the sound of your cry; when he hears it, he will answer you. Though the Lord may give you the bread of adversity and the water of affliction, yet your Teacher will not hide himself

14

any more, but your eyes shall see your Teacher. And when you turn to the right or when you turn to the left, your ears shall hear a word behind you, saying, "This is the way; walk in it."

He will give rain for the seed with which you sow the ground, and grain, the produce of the ground, which will be rich and plenteous. On that day your cattle will graze in broad pastures; and the oxen and donkeys that till the ground will eat silage, which has been winnowed with shovel and fork. On every lofty mountain and every high hill there will be brooks running with water—on a day of the great slaughter, when the towers fall. Moreover, the light of the moon will be like the light of the sun, and the light of the sun will be sevenfold, like the light of seven days, on the day when the Lord binds up the injuries of his people, and heals the wounds inflicted by his blow.

- Does the promise that God will be gracious to me in my distress touch a chord with me?

- Do I feel I have been given the "bread of adversity" and the "water of affliction"? Do I feel for others in their affliction?

- As I listen to the Lord's promises, in what space do they find me? Buoyant and responsive? Weighed down and cynical? Vulnerable?

- Wherever I am today can I hear the Lord's words of consolation and offer of guidance?

December 7–13, 2008

Something to think and pray about each day this week:

Blessed Expectation

In the last month of pregnancy, a young mother becomes more and more preoccupied with the child she carries. In Ireland she may hear the old blessing: "God be with you both." She is more careful of herself, of her food and drink, her habits, and the daily hazards of living. She feels the movement of the child in her, exploring its comfortable ambiance, and starting to listen to the sounds of the womb, the mother's heart-beat and the music and noises that penetrate to her womb. So it was in Nazareth, as Mary kept house and lived in expectation. This was how the Lord was entering our world, as Alice Meynell wrote:

> No sudden thing of glory and fear
> Was the Lord's coming; but the dear
> Slow Nature's days followed each other

To form the Saviour from His Mother
—One of the children of the year.

The Presence of God

God is with me, but more,
God is within me, giving me existence.
Let me dwell for a moment on God's life-giving presence
in my body, my mind, my heart
and in the whole of my life.

Freedom

God is not foreign to my freedom.
Instead the Spirit breathes life into my most intimate desires,
gently nudging me towards all that is good.
I ask for the grace to let myself be enfolded by the Spirit.

Consciousness

In God's loving presence I unwind the past day,
starting from now and looking back, moment by moment.
I gather in all the goodness and light, in gratitude.
I attend to the shadows and what they say to me,
seeking healing, courage, forgiveness.

The Word

I read the Word of God slowly, a few times over, and I listen to what God is saying to me. (Please turn to your scripture on the following pages. Inspiration points are there should you need them. When you are ready, return here to continue.)

Conversation

How has God's Word moved me? Has it left me cold?

Has it consoled me or moved me to act in a new way?

I imagine Jesus standing or sitting beside me,

I turn and share my feelings with him.

Conclusion

Glory be to the Father, and to the Son, and to the Holy Spirit,

As it was in the beginning, is now and ever shall be,

World without end. Amen

Sunday 7th December,
Second Sunday of Advent   Isaiah 40:1–5, 9–11

Comfort, O comfort my people, says your God. Speak tenderly to Jerusalem, and cry to her that she has served her term, that her penalty is paid, that she has received from the Lord's hand double for all her sins. A voice cries out: "In the wilderness prepare the way of the Lord, make straight in the desert a highway for our God. Every valley shall be lifted up, and every mountain and hill be made low; the uneven ground shall become level, and the rough places a plain. Then the glory of the Lord shall be revealed, and all people shall see it together, for the mouth of the Lord has spoken."

Get you up to a high mountain, O Zion, herald of good tidings; lift up your voice with strength, O Jerusalem, herald of good tidings, lift it up, do not fear; say to the cities of Judah, 'Here is your God!'

See, the Lord God comes with might, and his arm rules for him; his reward is with him, and his recompense before him. He will feed his flock like a shepherd; he will gather the lambs in his arms, and carry them in his bosom, and gently lead the mother sheep. How can I prepare the way for the Lord to enter more into my life?

- There was a time of retribution and punishment, but now is the time for reconciliation. God comes to me in mercy and tenderness.

- How can I prepare the way for the Lord to enter more into my life?

- Is there "uneven ground" or "rough places" in my life, where I don't really want to let God in? Listen to the first couple of sentences again: God comes to me in mercy and tenderness.

Monday 8th December, The Immaculate Conception of the Blessed Virgin Mary
Luke 1:26–38

I n the sixth month the angel Gabriel was sent by God to a town in Galilee called Nazareth, to a virgin engaged to a man whose name was Joseph, of the house of David. The virgin's name was Mary. And he came to her and said, "Greetings, favored one! The Lord is with you." But she was much perplexed by his words and pondered what sort of greeting this might be. The angel said to her, "Do not be afraid, Mary, for you have found favor with God. And now, you will conceive in your womb and bear a son, and you will name him Jesus. He will be great, and will be called the Son of the Most High, and the Lord God will give to him the throne of his ancestor David. He will reign over the house of Jacob forever, and of his kingdom there will be no end." Mary said to the angel, "How can this be, since I am a virgin?" The angel said to her, "The Holy Spirit will come upon you, and the power of the Most High will overshadow you; therefore the child to be born will be holy; he will be called Son of God. And now, your relative Elizabeth in her old age has also conceived a son; and this is the sixth month for her who was said to be barren. For nothing will be impossible with God." Then Mary said, "Here am I, the servant of the Lord; let it be with me according to your word." Then the angel departed from her.

- By her yes, Mary first bore the Son of God in her heart, and then in her body.

- Can I watch the scene? A young woman, who could have had no idea of what was being asked or where it might lead, made a leap of trust, of faith, and of hope.

- How does Mary's experience touch me? Am I called to "bear" God in my heart?

- What issues of surrender and trust arise in my case?

Tuesday 9th December   Isaiah 40:3–11

A voice cries out: "In the wilderness prepare the way of the Lord, make straight in the desert a highway for our God. Every valley shall be lifted up, and every mountain and hill be made low; the uneven ground shall become level, and the rough places a plain. Then the glory of the Lord shall be revealed, and all people shall see it together, for the mouth of the Lord has spoken." A voice says, 'Cry out!' And I said, 'What shall I cry?'

All people are grass, their constancy is like the flower of the field. The grass withers, the flower fades, when the breath of the Lord blows upon it; surely the people are grass. The grass withers, the flower fades; but the word of our God will stand for ever.

Get you up to a high mountain, O Zion, herald of good tidings; lift up your voice with strength, O Jerusalem, herald of good tidings, lift it up, do not fear; say to the cities of Judah, 'Here is your God!' See, the Lord God comes with might, and his arm rules for him; his reward is with him, and his recompense before him. He will feed his flock like a shepherd; he will gather the lambs in his arms, and carry them in his bosom, and gently lead the mother sheep.

- Lord, I make this prayer in Advent. My days may be short and cold, or long and hot; but I really struggle when my heart is arid and dark.

- What I pray for is not the tinsel and giddiness of Christmas, but a strengthening of my weak hands, firming of my feeble knees. I pray to be strong and to leave my fears in your hands.

Wednesday 10th December   Isaiah 40:25–31

To whom then will you compare me, or who is my equal? says the Holy One. Lift up your eyes on high and see: Who created these? He who brings out their host and numbers them, calling them all by name; because he is great in strength, mighty in power, not one is missing. Why do you say, O Jacob, and speak, O Israel, 'My way is hidden from the Lord, and my right is disregarded by my God'? Have you not known? Have you not heard? The Lord is the everlasting God, the Creator of the ends of the earth. He does not faint or grow weary; his understanding is unsearchable. He gives power to the faint, and strengthens the powerless. Even youths will faint and be weary, and the young will fall exhausted; but those who wait for the Lord shall renew their strength, they shall mount up with wings like eagles, they shall run and not be weary, they shall walk and not faint.

- The words of the Lord are like the eagle's wings, words that soar, words that cut through, words of great power and strength.

- Can I deepen my hope in God by giving more attention and time to these words? Can these words become part of my very being?

Thursday 11th December   Matthew 11:11–15

Truly I tell you, among those born of women no one has arisen greater than John the Baptist; yet the least in the kingdom of heaven is greater than he. From the days of John the Baptist until now the kingdom of heaven has suffered violence, and the violent take it by force. For all the prophets and the law prophesied until John came; and if you are willing to accept it, he is Elijah who is to come. Let anyone with ears listen!

- How are we to understand what Jesus says to us here? On one hand, John is a great man; there is none greater. On the other hand, he ranks below the very least who are in the kingdom.

- Can I focus on this kingdom Jesus speaks of? Or am I distracted by what is around me? Am I really listening to his message?

Friday 12th December   **Matthew 11:16–19**

Jesus spoke to the crowds, "But to what will I compare this generation? It is like children sitting in the marketplaces and calling to one another, 'We played the flute for you, and you did not dance; we wailed, and you did not mourn.' For John came neither eating nor drinking, and they say, 'He has a demon'; the Son of Man came eating and drinking, and they say, 'Look, a glutton and a drunkard, a friend of tax collectors and sinners!' Yet wisdom is vindicated by her deeds."

• In this frustrated comment of Jesus, we have some sense of how people saw him. In contrast to John the Baptist, he ate and drank like the common man, and his friends were considered disreputable. From the beginning of his public life, those who did not believe in Jesus' preaching or his miracles discerned nothing of the divine in his features. He was too ordinary.

• Lord, I take comfort in your ordinariness. May I find you in what is workaday, ordinary, and routine.

Saturday 13th December   Matthew 17: 9a,10–13

As they were coming down the mountain, the disciples asked Jesus, "Why, then, do the scribes say that Elijah must come first?" He replied, "Elijah is indeed coming and will restore all things; but I tell you that Elijah has already come, and they did not recognize him, but they did to him whatever they pleased. So also the Son of Man is about to suffer at their hands." Then the disciples understood that he was speaking to them about John the Baptist.

- God's messengers tend to be rejected. This is a bitter truth about our human condition in the midst of our Advent journey. Advent still calls us to a fulfillment promised and guaranteed by God.

- In my prayer can I hold together both the promise and the shadow?

December 14–20, 2008

Something to think and pray about each day this week:

God's Refugees

Like any young couple planning together, Mary and Joseph would have given thought to the coming birth in Nazareth: what friend or neighbor would be the midwife, how they would prepare the room and the house. But in the weeks before the birth, menacing rumors reached them of a census that would force them away from home. Quiet, imperturbable Joseph had to make travel plans. We think of him walking, with his pregnant wife on a donkey, up the ninety miles to Jerusalem and Bethlehem. The last part of the journey was a climb into the hills of Judea. But more stressful than the journey was the uncertainty. Where will we sleep? How can I care for Mary in her condition? What does God mean by putting us through this? He and Mary and her child were in the condition of refugees the world over. In that winter season it was a question not of shopping but of survival. In this season we try to open our hearts to the refugees of our time.

The Presence of God

What is present to me is what has a hold on my becoming.
I reflect on the presence of God always there in love, amidst the many things that have a hold on me.
I pause and pray that I may let God affect my becoming in this precise moment.

Freedom

There are very few people
who realize what God would make of them
if they abandoned themselves into his hands,
and let themselves be formed by his grace.
I ask for the grace to trust myself totally to God's love.

Consciousness

I exist in a web of relationships—links to nature, people, God.
I trace out these links, giving thanks for the life that flows through them.
Some links are twisted or broken: I may feel regret, anger, disappointment.
I pray for the gift of acceptance and forgiveness.

The Word

God speaks to each one of us individually. I need to listen to hear what he is saying to me. Read the text a few times, then listen. (Please turn to your scripture on the following pages. Inspiration points are there should you need them. When you are ready, return here to continue.)

Conversation

What is stirring in me as I pray?
Am I consoled, troubled, left cold?
I imagine Jesus himself standing or sitting at my side,
and share my feelings with him.

Conclusion

Glory be to the Father, and to the Son, and to the Holy Spirit,
As it was in the beginning, is now and ever shall be,
World without end. Amen

Sunday 14th December,
Third Sunday of Advent   Isaiah 61:1–2,10–11

The spirit of the Lord God is upon me, because the Lord has anointed me; he has sent me to bring good news to the oppressed, to bind up the brokenhearted, to proclaim liberty to the captives, and release to the prisoners; to proclaim the year of the Lord's favor, and the day of vengeance of our God . . . I will greatly rejoice in the Lord, my whole being shall exult in my God; for he has clothed me with the garments of salvation, he has covered me with the robe of righteousness, as a bridegroom decks himself with a garland, and as a bride adorns herself with her jewels. For as the earth brings forth its shoots, and as a garden causes what is sown in it to spring up, so the Lord God will cause righteousness and praise to spring up before all the nations.

- These are the words of Isaiah, God's servant. Jesus applied them to himself. They apply to us, too, as Christians.

- God speaks to us here and asks us to "proclaim the year of the Lord's favor." How am I going to respond? What am I going to do to make 2009 a year when people experience the love of

God and are freed from captivity, oppression, and heartbreak?

*   If I think I can do nothing, listen to God's promise: The Lord will make justice spring up as surely as what is sown springs up from a garden.

Monday 15th December   Matthew 21:23–27

When Jesus entered the temple, the chief priests and the elders of the people came to him as he was teaching, and said, "By what authority are you doing these things, and who gave you this authority?" Jesus said to them, "I will also ask you one question; if you tell me the answer, then I will also tell you by what authority I do these things. Did the baptism of John come from heaven, or was it of human origin?" And they argued with one another, "If we say, 'From heaven,' he will say to us, 'Why then did you not believe him?' But if we say, 'Of human origin,' we are afraid of the crowd; for all regard John as a prophet." So they answered Jesus, "We do not know." And he said to them, "Neither will I tell you by what authority I am doing these things."

- In this exchange, Jesus might look as if he is playing a cheap trick on the chief priests and elders. But notice the differences between them.

- The chief priests and the elders are motivated both by a desire to protect their own position and authority, and by fear—they are afraid of the crowds. Jesus, on the other hand, always speaks out fearlessly, regardless of how it might jeopardize his popularity.

- Do I let fear run my life? Do I make decisions on the basis of preserving my position and power? Can I talk to Jesus about this and ask for the grace to be free, as he was?

Tuesday 16th December   Matthew 21:28–32

Jesus said, "What do you think? A man had two sons; he went to the first and said, 'Son, go and work in the vineyard today.' He answered, 'I will not'; but later he changed his mind and went. The father went to the second and said the same; and he answered, 'I go, sir'; but he did not go. Which of the two did the will of his father?" They said, "The first." Jesus said to them, "Truly I tell you, the tax collectors and the prostitutes are going into the kingdom of God ahead of you. For John came to you in the way of righteousness and you did not believe him, but the tax collectors and the prostitutes believed him; and even after you saw it, you did not change your minds and believe him."

- The first son sounds like a grump, hard to live with. His first reaction tended to be No. He and others probably suffered from his grumpiness but you could still trust him to help. The second son was a charmer; he flattered but deceived his father. When he should have been working, he found something better to do.

- Lord, I would rather be a grumpy but reliable helper than a sweet-talking charmer.

Wednesday 17th December   Matthew 1:1–17

An account of the genealogy of Jesus the Messiah, the son of David, the son of Abraham. Abraham was the father of Isaac, and Isaac the father of Jacob, and Jacob the father of Judah and his brothers, and Judah the father of Perez and Zerah by Tamar, and Perez the father of Hezron, and Hezron the father of Aram, and Aram the father of Aminadab, and Aminadab the father of Nahshon, and

Nahshon the father of Salmon, and Salmon the father of Boaz by Rahab, and Boaz the father of Obed by Ruth, and Obed the father of Jesse, and Jesse the father of King David. And David was the father of Solomon by the wife of Uriah, and Solomon the father of Rehoboam, and Rehoboam the father of Abijah, and Abijah the father of Asaph, and Asaph the father of Jehoshaphat, and Jehoshaphat the father of Joram, and Joram the father of Uzziah, and Uzziah the father of Jotham, and Jotham the father of Ahaz, and Ahaz the father of Hezekiah, and Hezekiah the father of Manasseh, and Manasseh the father of Amos, and Amos the father of Josiah, and Josiah the father of Jechoniah and his brothers, at the time of the deportation to Babylon. And after the deportation to Babylon: Jechoniah was the father of Salathiel, and Salathiel the father of Zerubbabel, and Zerubbabel the father of Abiud, and Abiud the father of Eliakim, and Eliakim the father of Azor, and Azor the father of Zadok, and Zadok the father of Achim, and Achim the father of Eliud, and Eliud the father of Eleazar, and Eleazar the father of Matthan, and Matthan the father of Jacob, and Jacob the father of Joseph the husband of Mary, of whom Jesus was born, who is called the

36

Messiah. So all the generations from Abraham to
David are fourteen generations; and from David to
the deportation to Babylon, fourteen generations;
and from the deportation to Babylon to the Messiah, fourteen generations.

- This is more than a list of biblical names: Matthew is rattling skeletons in the cupboard of
  Jesus' ancestry. He includes four controversial
  mothers with his list of fathers. Tamar dressed as
  a prostitute and bore twins to her father-in-law.
  Rahab betrayed her city. Ruth was a Gentile.
  Solomon was the child of David's adulterous
  affair with Bathsheba.

- There is no airbrushing of Jesus' pedigree: He
  comes to us laden with all the disreputable past
  of his race and shows how each birth is a fresh
  beginning.

- How do I regard the "wayward" ones in my
  family tree or treat the embarrassing relatives I
  have? Lord, teach me to accept my humanity,
  my genes, my relatives, as you did.

Thursday 18th December   Jeremiah 23:5–8

The days are surely coming, says the Lord, when I will raise up for David a righteous Branch, and he shall reign as king and deal wisely, and shall execute justice and righteousness in the land. In his days Judah will be saved and Israel will live in safety. And this is the name by which he will be called: "The Lord is our righteousness."

Therefore, the days are surely coming, says the Lord, when it shall no longer be said, 'As the Lord lives who brought the people of Israel up out of the land of Egypt', but 'As the Lord lives who brought out and led the offspring of the house of Israel out of the land of the north and out of all the lands where he had driven them.' Then they shall live in their own land.

- When speaking about the future of Israel, the prophets remind us of God's great works in the past.

- By looking back in meditation I can look forward in expectation; by holding on to the memory of Jesus' birth, I can progress towards the kingdom.

- During this Advent, Lord, lead me to deepen my memory of God's great deeds for his people so I look forward with courage.

Friday 19th December   Judges 13:2–7, 24–25

There was a certain man of Zorah, of the tribe of the Danites, whose name was Manoah. His wife was barren, having borne no children. And the angel of the Lord appeared to the woman and said to her, "Although you are barren, having borne no children, you shall conceive and bear a son. Now be careful not to drink wine or strong drink, or to eat anything unclean, for you shall conceive and bear a son. No razor is to come on his head, for the boy shall be a nazirite to God from birth. It is he who shall begin to deliver Israel from the hand of the Philistines." Then the woman came and told her husband, "A man of God came to me, and his appearance was like that of an angel of God, most awe-inspiring; I did not ask him where he came from, and he did not tell me his name; but he said to me, 'You shall conceive and bear a son. So then drink no wine or strong drink, and eat nothing unclean, for the boy shall be a nazirite to God from birth to the day of his death.'" The woman bore a son, and named him Samson. The boy grew, and the Lord blessed him. The spirit of the Lord began to stir him in Mahaneh-dan, between Zorah and Eshtaol.

- The readings this week are about fertility and birth, often against the odds. New-born children can seem a miracle to their parents, who marvel at the power of new life which has flowed through them.

- Lord, open me to the new life which you promise at Christmas. Are there areas of "barrenness" in my life where I might be open to being surprised?

Saturday 20th December   **Isaiah 7:10–14**

Again the Lord spoke to Ahaz, saying, "Ask a sign of the Lord your God; let it be deep as Sheol or high as heaven." But Ahaz said, "I will not ask, and I will not put the Lord to the test." Then Isaiah said: "Hear then, O house of David! Is it too little for you to weary mortals, that you weary my God also? Therefore the Lord himself will give you a sign. Look, the young woman is with child and shall bear a son, and shall name him Immanuel."

- As we build towards the great event of the birth of the Son of God, it is good to remember the prophecy given long before by the prophet Isaiah: "the young woman is with child . . ."

- Can I situate myself in the great sweep of history where God planned from the beginning to take on flesh and share our lot, my lot?

- Immanuel means "God is with us." How is that true for me?

Fourth Week of Advent/Christmas
December 21–27, 2008

Something to think and pray about each day this week:

The Little One

As Mary's time drew near, the situation grew more baffling and distressing. Even the shelters which Joseph had budgeted for, the wayside inns, turned them away: no vacancies. In children's Christmas plays, the inn-keeper is played variously as cruel and uncaring, or as concerned but unable to help, other than by offering a stable. It is there that we have one of the most familiar and loved scenes in human history, the manger in Bethlehem, as Sartre pictured it:

> The Virgin is pale, and she looks at the baby. What I would paint on her face is an anxious wonderment, such as has never before been seen on a human face. For Christ is her baby, flesh of her flesh, and the fruit of her womb. She has carried him for nine

months, and she will give him her breast,
and her milk will become the blood of
God. There are moments when the temptation is so strong that she forgets that he
is God. She folds him in her arms and says:
My little one.

The Presence of God
God is with me, but more, God is within me.
Let me dwell for a moment on God's life-giving
presence
in my body, in my mind, in my heart,
as I sit here, right now.

Freedom
A thick and shapeless tree-trunk would never
believe
that it could become a statue, admired as a miracle
of sculpture,
and would never submit itself to the chisel of the
sculptor,
who sees by her genius what she can make of it.
(St Ignatius)
I ask for the grace to let myself be shaped by my
loving Creator.

Consciousness

Knowing that God loves me unconditionally,
I can afford to be honest about how I am.
How has the last day been, and how do I feel now?
I share my feelings openly with the Lord.

The Word

I read the Word of God slowly, a few times over,
and I listen to what God is saying to me. (Please
turn to your scripture on the following pages. Inspiration points are there should you need them.
When you are ready, return here to continue.)

Conversation

Do I notice myself reacting as I pray with the
Word of God?
Do I feel challenged, comforted, angry?
Imagining Jesus sitting or standing by me,
I speak out my feelings, as one trusted friend to
another.

Conclusion

Glory be to the Father, and to the Son, and to the
Holy Spirit,
As it was in the beginning, is now and ever shall
be,
World without end. Amen

Sunday 21st December,
Fourth Sunday of Advent   Luke 1:26–38

I n the sixth month the angel Gabriel was sent by God to a town in Galilee called Nazareth, to a virgin engaged to a man whose name was Joseph, of the house of David. The virgin's name was Mary. And he came to her and said, 'Greetings, favored one! The Lord is with you.' But she was much perplexed by his words and pondered what sort of greeting this might be. The angel said to her, 'Do not be afraid, Mary, for you have found favor with God. And now, you will conceive in your womb and bear a son, and you will name him Jesus. He will be great, and will be called the Son of the Most High, and the Lord God will give to him the throne of his ancestor David. He will reign over the house of Jacob for ever, and of his kingdom there will be no end.' Mary said to the angel, 'How can this be, since I am a virgin?' The angel said to her, 'The Holy Spirit will come upon you, and the power of the Most High will overshadow you; therefore the child to be born will be holy; he will be called Son of God. And now, your relative Elizabeth in her old age has also conceived a son; and this is the sixth month for her who was said to be barren. For nothing will be impossible with God.' Then Mary said, 'Here am I, the servant of the Lord; let it be with me according to your word.' Then the angel departed from her.

- Imagine what Mary felt as she was given this awesome news.

- Mary has questions, and she voices them, but she says "Yes" to God's will for her. Can I learn from her example?

Monday 22nd December   Luke 1:46–56

And Mary said, "My soul magnifies the Lord, and my spirit rejoices in God my Savior, for he has looked with favor on the lowliness of his servant. Surely, from now on all generations will call me blessed; for the Mighty One has done great things for me, and holy is his name. His mercy is for those who fear him from generation to generation. He has shown strength with his arm; he has scattered the proud in the thoughts of their hearts. He has brought down the powerful from their thrones, and lifted up the lowly; he has filled the hungry with good things, and sent the rich away empty.

He has helped his servant Israel, in remembrance of his mercy, according to the promise he made to our ancestors, to Abraham and to his descendants forever." And Mary remained with Elizabeth about three months and then returned to her home.

- The *Magnificat*, as we call Mary's prayer, has become our traditional hymn of gratitude and joy. This is a moment of ecstatic fulfillment, when Mary looks back on all the promises of the Old Testament and begins to sense and relish her own role in the Lord's plan.

- Can I pray the *Magnificat* in gratitude for God's goodness to me?

Tuesday 23rd December   Luke 1:57–66

Now the time came for Elizabeth to give birth, and she bore a son. Her neighbors and relatives heard that the Lord had shown his great mercy to her, and they rejoiced with her. On the eighth day they came to circumcise the child, and they were going to name him Zechariah after his father. But his mother said, "No; he is to be called John." They said to her, "None of your relatives has this name." Then they began motioning to his father to find out what name he wanted to give him. He asked for a writing tablet and wrote, "His name is John." And all of them were amazed. Immediately his mouth was opened and his tongue freed, and he began to speak, praising God. Fear came over all their neighbors, and all these things were talked about throughout the entire hill country of Judea. All who heard them pondered them and said, "What then will this child become?" For, indeed, the hand of the Lord was with him.

- "He is to be called John." He is in God's favor. Each one of us has received a name and is known by a name. As a parent, we may also have given a name to our own child and wondered "What then will this child become?"

- God favors me and knows me by my name. Can I give thanks for those who named me, for the hopes that others have for me, for each person who knows my name?

Wednesday 24th December Luke 1:67–79

Then his father Zechariah was filled with the Holy Spirit and spoke this prophecy: "Blessed be the Lord God of Israel, for he has looked favorably on his people and redeemed them. He has raised up a mighty savior for us in the house of his servant David, as he spoke through the mouth of his holy prophets from of old, that we would be saved from our enemies and from the hand of all who hate us. Thus he has shown the mercy promised to our ancestors, and has remembered his holy covenant, the oath that he swore to our ancestor Abraham, to grant us that we, being rescued from the hands of our enemies, might serve him without fear, in holiness and righteousness before him all our days. And you, child, will be called the prophet of the Most High; for you will go before the Lord to prepare his ways, to give knowledge of salvation to his people by the forgiveness of their sins. By the tender mercy of our God, the dawn from on high will break upon us, to give light to those who sit in darkness and in the shadow of death, to guide our feet into the way of peace."

- "By the tender mercy of our God." Our God has such a long history of "tender mercy" towards his people, a constant invitation to each of us, culminating in the gift of an infant Son.

- Am I ready this Christmas to invite Jesus into my heart and my home, giving all that I have over to him?

Thursday 25th December, Feast of the Nativity of the Lord   Luke 2:6–14

While they were in Bethlehem, the time came for Mary to deliver her child. And she gave birth to her firstborn son and wrapped him in bands of cloth, and laid him in a manger, because there was no place for them in the inn. In that region there were shepherds living in the fields, keeping watch over their flock by night. Then an angel of the Lord stood before them, and the glory of the Lord shone around them, and they were terrified. But the angel said to them, "Do not be afraid; for see—I am bringing you good news of great joy for all the people: to you is born this day in the city of David a Savior, who is the Messiah, the Lord. This will be a sign for you: you will find a child wrapped in bands of cloth and lying in a manger." And suddenly there was with the angel a multitude of the heavenly host, praising God and saying, "Glory to God in the highest heaven, and on earth peace among those whom he favors!"

- "And she gave birth to her first-born son." A normal, everyday event with ordinary people gathered together—but this birth in Bethlehem was one to shake the world. This baby is the Son of God, the Savior of the world.

- What is God doing here, among us? How do I care for this child in the manger?

Friday 26th December, St. Stephen, the First Martyr   Matthew 10:17–22

Jesus said to his apostles, "Beware of them, for they will hand you over to councils and flog you in their synagogues; and you will be dragged before governors and kings because of me, as a testimony to them and the Gentiles. When they hand you over, do not worry about how you are to speak or what you are to say; for what you are to say will be given to you at that time; for it is not you who speak, but the Spirit of your Father speaking through you. Brother will betray brother to death, and a father his child, and children will rise against parents and have them put to death; and you will be hated by all because of my name. But the one who endures to the end will be saved."

- Pope John Paul II wrote that the best word to describe *agape*, or perfect Christian love, is "solidarity"—a word for hanging in, despite brokenness in ourselves and others, for letting love lead us where it will, even to being willing to pay the price.

- Lord, when I close my eyes for the last time, may I have purged all my resentments and forgiven any enemies; and may I see your face.

Saturday 27th December, St. John, Apostle and Evangelist   John 20:2–8

So Mary Magdalene ran and went to Simon Peter and the other disciple, the one whom Jesus loved, and said to them, "They have taken the Lord out of the tomb, and we do not know where they have laid him." Then Peter and the other disciple set out and went toward the tomb. The two were running together, but the other disciple outran Peter and reached the tomb first. He bent down to look in and saw the linen wrappings lying there, but he did not go in. Then Simon Peter came, following him, and went into the tomb. He saw the linen wrappings lying there, and the cloth that had been on Jesus' head, not lying with the linen wrappings but rolled up in a place by itself. Then the other disciple, who reached the tomb first, also went in, and he saw and believed.

- This gospel for St. John's feast refers to him only as the other disciple, the one whom Jesus loved. It is a moment of unalloyed joy, as John and Peter grapple with the fact of Jesus risen from the dead. They move from concern with burial cloths and an empty tomb, to a realization that death had met its master; the one whom they loved was with them for ever.

- How does this affect me, today? Can I move beyond my immediate concerns, towards what is really important?

December 28, 2008–January 4, 2009

Something to think and pray about each day this week:

Endings and Beginnings

As my year draws to a close, I look back at its mixture of joyful and sorrowful episodes, some times that were boring, others exciting or deeply moving. Where was the love in my life this year? Has the year 2008 left me with any unresolved angers or resentments? How can I go into 2009 with a peaceful and clean heart? Where was God in all the personal experiences which leap into my memory? Did I recognize him in them at the time? Can I work through them now in my prayer?

May the favor of God be upon me in 2009.

The Presence of God

As I sit here, the beating of my heart,
the ebb and flow of my breathing, the movements
of my mind
are all signs of God's ongoing creation of me.

I pause for a moment, and become aware
of this presence of God within me.

Freedom

I ask for the grace
to let go of my own concerns
and be open to what God is asking of me,
to let myself be guided and formed by my loving
Creator.

Consciousness

In the presence of my loving Creator,
I look honestly at my feelings over the last day,
the highs, the lows, and the level ground.
Can I see where the Lord has been present?

The Word

I take my time to read the Word of God, slowly,
a few times, allowing myself to dwell on anything
that strikes me. (Please turn to your scripture on
the following pages. Inspiration points are there
should you need them. When you are ready, return here to continue.)

Conversation

Remembering that I am still in God's presence,
I imagine Jesus himself standing or sitting beside
me,

and say whatever is on my mind, whatever is in
my heart,
speaking as one friend to another.

Conclusion

Glory be to the Father, and to the Son, and to the
Holy Spirit,
As it was in the beginning, is now and ever shall be,
World without end. Amen

Sunday 28th December,
The Holy Family   Colossians 3:12–21

As God's chosen ones, holy and beloved, clothe yourselves with compassion, kindness, humility, meekness, and patience. Bear with one another and, if anyone has a complaint against another, forgive each other; just as the Lord has forgiven you, so you also must forgive. Above all, clothe yourselves with love, which binds everything together in perfect harmony. And let the peace of Christ rule in your hearts, to which indeed you were called in the one body. And be thankful. Let the word of Christ dwell in you richly; teach and admonish one another in all wisdom; and with gratitude in your hearts sing psalms, hymns, and spiritual songs to God. And whatever you do, in word or deed, do everything in the name of the Lord Jesus, giving thanks to God the Father through him. Wives, be subject to your husbands, as is fitting in the Lord. Husbands, love your wives and never treat them harshly. Children, obey your parents in everything, for this is your acceptable duty in the Lord. Fathers, do not provoke your children, or they may lose heart.

- "Bear with one another . . . forgive each other."
  We can focus on all the "holy" words that Paul
  uses here—compassion; kindness; humility;
  meekness; perfect harmony"—but what often
  troubles us in our daily lives is putting up with
  each other. We can feel deep failure in our relationships with those who are close to us.

- At the core of each marriage and strong relationship is the union: We are together. Don't
  question that; God certainly doesn't. We can
  fall out along the way, but we are always wel-
  comed back into this union.

- This is a wonderful and powerful image of the
  way God loves us: God just won't let go of us.
  Let us give thanks and forgive one another.

Monday 29th December   Luke 2:25–35

Now there was a man in Jerusalem whose name
was Simeon; this man was righteous and devout, looking forward to the consolation of Israel,
and the Holy Spirit rested on him. It had been revealed to him by the Holy Spirit that he would not
see death before he had seen the Lord's Messiah.
Guided by the Spirit, Simeon came into the temple;

and when the parents brought in the child Jesus, to do for him what was customary under the law, Simeon took him in his arms and praised God, saying, "Master, now you are dismissing your servant in peace, according to your word; for my eyes have seen your salvation, which you have prepared in the presence of all peoples, a light for revelation to the Gentiles and for glory to your people Israel." And the child's father and mother were amazed at what was being said about him. Then Simeon blessed them and said to his mother Mary, 'This child is destined for the falling and the rising of many in Israel, and to be a sign that will be opposed so that the inner thoughts of many will be revealed—and a sword will pierce your own soul too.'

- All his life, Simeon had been waiting and hoping. Now the Incarnate God lives! Now, filled with the Spirit, he utters his song of praise we call the *Nunc Dimittis*.

- What did Simeon see in this ordinary family's child? How did he see it? Do I see it?

- Can I join with Simeon in his song?

Tuesday 30th December   **Luke 2:36–40**

There was also a prophet, Anna the daughter of Phanuel, of the tribe of Asher. She was of a great age, having lived with her husband seven years after her marriage, then as a widow to the age of eighty-four. She never left the temple but worshiped there with fasting and prayer night and day. At that moment she came, and began to praise God and to speak about the child to all who were looking for the redemption of Jerusalem. When they had finished everything required by the law of the Lord, they returned to Galilee, to their own town of Nazareth. The child grew and became strong, filled with wisdom; and the favor of God was upon him.

- Anna, a prophet in the Old Testament tradition like Simeon, recognizes that salvation has come in this child. Anna speaks up.

- What did Anna see in this ordinary family's child? How did she see it? Do I see it?

Wednesday 31st December   **John 1:1–18**

In the beginning was the Word, and the Word was with God, and the Word was God. He was in the beginning with God. All things came into being through him, and without him not one thing came into being. What has come into being in him was life, and the life was the light of all people. The light shines in the darkness, and the darkness did not overcome it. There was a man sent from God, whose name was John. He came as a witness to testify to the light, so that all might believe through him. He himself was not the light, but he came to testify to the light. The true light, which enlightens everyone, was coming into the world. He was in the world, and the world came into being through him; yet the world did not know him. He came to what was his own, and his own people did not accept him. But to all who received him, who believed in his name, he gave power to become children of God, who were born, not of blood or of the will of the flesh or of the will of man, but of God. And the Word became flesh and lived among us, and we have seen his glory, the glory as of a father's only son, full of grace and truth. (John testified to him and cried out, "This was he of whom I said, 'He who comes after me ranks ahead of me because he was before me.'") From his fullness we have all received, grace upon grace. The law indeed was given through Moses; grace and truth came through Jesus Christ. No one has ever seen God. It is God the only Son, who is close to the Father's heart, who has made him known.

- This is the truth around which the fourth Gospel was written: that in Jesus, God has broken his immemorial silence. His Word, the perfect reflection of his Godhead, has become flesh in Jesus.

- We look at Jesus, see him grow and change, and wonder at the grace and truth that shine in and through him. Lord, let me continue to receive from your fullness.

Thursday 1st January, Solemnity of Mary, Mother of God   Luke 2:15–21

When the angels had left them and gone into heaven, the shepherds said to one another, "Let us go now to Bethlehem and see this thing that has taken place, which the Lord has made known to us." So they went with haste and found Mary and Joseph, and the child lying in the manger. When they saw this, they made known what had been told them about this child; and all who heard it were amazed at what the shepherds told them. But Mary treasured all these words and pondered them in her heart. The shepherds returned, glorifying and praising God for all they had heard and seen, as it had been told them. After eight days had passed, it was time to circumcise the child; and he was called Jesus, the name given by the angel before he was conceived in the womb.

• For centuries Christians tried to put words on Mary's relationship with God, and with the Council of Ephesus they affirmed that she can rightly be called Mother of God, the feast that is celebrated today. We may still struggle to find the right words to describe this mystery, but more easily contemplate Mary at the crib, as described by Sartre in his Christmas play, *Barjona*:

> There are rapid, fleeting moments when Mary realizes at once that Christ is her son, her very own baby, and that he is

God. She looks at him and thinks: "This God is my baby. This divine flesh is my flesh. He is made from me. He has my eyes, and the curve of his mouth is the curve of mine. He is like me. He is God and he is like me."

Friday 2nd January   John 1:19–28

This is the testimony given by John when the Jews sent priests and Levites from Jerusalem to ask him, "Who are you?" He confessed and did not deny it, but confessed, "I am not the Messiah." And they asked him, "What then? Are you Elijah?" He said, "I am not." "Are you the prophet?" He answered, "No." Then they said to him, "Who are you? Let us have an answer for those who sent us. What do you say about yourself?" He said, "I am the voice of one crying out in the wilderness, 'Make straight the way of the Lord,'" as the prophet Isaiah said. Now they had been sent from the Pharisees. They asked him, "Why then are you baptizing if you are neither the Messiah, nor Elijah, nor the prophet?" John answered them, "I baptize with water. Among you stands one whom you do not know, the one who is coming after me; I am not worthy to untie the thong of his sandal." This took place in Bethany across the Jordan where John was baptizing.

- There is a question for me: "Who are you? . . . What do you say about yourself?"

- Lord, I think of you beside me, seeing the good and the promise in me. This is what I want to say about myself: I am called into being by God, who loves me.

Saturday 3rd January John 1:29–34

The next day John saw Jesus coming toward him and declared, "Here is the Lamb of God who takes away the sin of the world! This is he of whom I said, 'After me comes a man who ranks ahead of me because he was before me.' I myself did not know him; but I came baptizing with water for this reason, that he might be revealed to Israel." And John testified, "I saw the Spirit descending from heaven like a dove, and it remained on him. I myself did not know him, but the one who sent me to baptize with water said to me, 'He on whom you see the Spirit descend and remain is the one who baptizes with the Holy Spirit.' And I myself have seen and have testified that this is the Son of God."

- "Lamb of God" stirs biblical images in us: of the Passover lamb, and of the Suffering Servant in Isaiah, led like a lamb to the slaughter, bearing our sins.

- Lord, whenever I hear of atrocious barbarism committed by one of our race, and of the injustice and pain which people suffer through others' wickedness, I remember that this is the same world you entered, the burden you took on yourself. You had a strong back to carry the evil that is in the world.

Sunday, 4th January,
The Epiphany of the Lord   Matthew 2:1–12

In the time of King Herod, after Jesus was born in Bethlehem of Judea, wise men from the East came to Jerusalem, asking, "Where is the child who has been born king of the Jews? For we observed his star at its rising, and have come to pay him homage." When King Herod heard this, he was frightened, and all Jerusalem with him; and calling together all the chief priests and scribes of the people, he inquired of them where the Messiah was to be born. They told him, "In Bethlehem of Judea; for so it has been written by the prophet: 'And you, Bethlehem, in the land of Judah, are by no means least among the rulers of Judah; for from you shall come a ruler who is to shepherd my people Israel.'" Then Herod secretly called for the wise men and learned from them the exact time when the star had appeared. Then he sent them to Bethlehem, saying, "Go and search diligently for the child; and when you have found him, bring me word so that I may also go and pay him homage." When they had heard the king, they set out; and there, ahead of them, went the star that they had seen at its rising, until it stopped over the place where the child was. When they saw that the star had stopped, they were overwhelmed with joy. On entering the house, they saw the child with Mary his mother; and they knelt down and paid him homage. Then, opening their treasure chests, they offered him gifts of gold, frankincense, and myrrh. And having been warned in a dream not to return to Herod, they left for their own country by another road.

- As Jesus' life begins to unfold for us, the gospel writers underline that Jesus was excluded: born "outside," in a stable; acclaimed as a king but immediately under threat from those who held political power.

- The three wise men are also outsiders; they are our spiritual forebears; through them we are invited to approach the Messiah.

- Lord, teach me to recognize God's children, and welcome them.

An Advent Retreat Day
Introduction to the Retreat

Welcome to this Advent retreat—a retreat that you can make in your own way and time.

A retreat is the name for putting aside time for God. It involves leaving some things in order to be present to Someone. God is always working with us, gently urging, communicating, and seeking contact, and our job is to give time to listen to the "message," whatever that message is!

Prayer is simply "being real with God" and letting God "in" to our often messy reality. Listening to the desires of our heart (God is in our deepest desires) means becoming quiet within, taking a step back, allowing things to surface, and listening to the "inner voice." It is like a pool where the water, when it is agitated and churned up, makes it impossible to see into the depths. Whereas when the water becomes calm and unruffled, it is possible to see. Hence the need for silence, "retreat," and time away.

You need to plan the day's retreat, combining the freedom of your own style with certain practical essentials for a meeting with God—or rather opening yourself to God who is present to you all the time. The most important thing is your own desire: an openness and a willingness to be available to God's stirrings in your interior and giving the time and energy to it. Also, just simply slowing down and "retreating" from the world is difficult, sometimes boring and seemingly pointless; yet the rewards if you stick with it are enormous! The goal is to live life more fully, engage with life totally and find that happiness that comes from following God's will.

Suggestions for preparing for the retreat:

Leave!

Leave aside work that is on your desk, you will come back to it more refreshed.

If you can, leave the phone off or off the hook. You may be able to leave your house if you are able to get to somewhere more helpful to pray. If not, you can create a space, putting newspapers and magazines to one side and leaving off the radio and television for a while. On a retreat we seek to break with noisy words to listen to the Word of God.

Change!

Change your routine! Re-arrange the room if you are staying put. If you are going out, perhaps you might walk somewhere different. It may be helpful to drop in to a different church for some time. This helps to create a sense of difference and avoids the places where people might ordinarily meet you. The external changes are to help us change within, to dispose ourselves to listen to God. Most importantly, let go of negative thoughts that might slip in—thoughts like, "It's not worth the effort!"

Plan!

It is helpful to think ahead about the shape of the day. Plan an adaptable schedule to include some relaxation or physical exercise to begin, times of prayer, a separate time to reflect on what it was like. It may be helpful to make a note of how you felt and what stays with you. We suggest three times of prayer and reflection: either over one day or over three days. It may be best to fix your time of prayer beforehand, e.g. 30, 40, 50, 60 minutes. Keep to that time! Avoid making subsequent prayer times shorter than the time you first chose.

Advent: Considering the Season

Advent is that time when all the Christian churches invite us to prepare to celebrate the "Coming of the Lord" among us. We don't only recall his coming in the past in Bethlehem, but anticipate his future coming. We are concerned not just with his coming in glory at the end of time, but his coming now into our lives. In Advent we remember his coming in history, we look forward to his coming in majesty, and we welcome his coming in mystery into our lives. Saint Matthew refers to the newborn Jesus as "Emmanuel, God with us." He ends his gospel with the promise of Jesus to his disciples: "Know that I will be with you always until the end of time." In Advent we celebrate the God who is ever coming, ever wanting to make his home not in a stable but in our hearts. In Advent we are invited to renew our faith in the Lord who comes, and to renew our faith in this Lord whose coming in Bethlehem is a concrete sign of his desire to come and make his home among us once again. As we make space for him we become instruments in his hands, witnesses to his hidden presence in our world.

Suggested Timetable

This timetable may be of help. You may find it better to use the sessions on different days as well.

9:30 am   *Preparation*: Take the time to prepare the place, the passage and your heart; maybe write some hopes for your day ("What do I really want?")

10:00 am   *Session 1*: Scripture: She wrapped him in swaddling clothes and laid him in a manger (Luke 2:1-7)

11:00 am   *Midmorning Break*: Take a stretch, go outside, have some refreshment

11:30 am   *Session 2*: Scripture: Prompted by the Spirit he came to the Temple (Luke 2:25-32)

12:30 pm   *Lunch Break*: Have a light meal, get a walk

2:30 pm   *Session 3*: Scripture: So stay awake, because you do not know when the master of the house is coming (Mark 13:33-37)

3:30 pm   *Afternoon Break*: Stretch, walk, relax

4:00 pm   *Review of the Day*: Look back to see where the moments of light and life were, acknowledging moments of darkness or difficulty without judging yourself. Writing this down can often help capture it.

Scripture: Luke 2:1–7

Take some time in prayer to look back and ponder on the birth of Jesus in Bethlehem.

Suggestion for beginning your time of prayer:

Presence of God:
For a few moments, or even longer, imagine how God sees you. Father, Son, and Holy Spirit each rejoice at your desire to give this time to prayer. Pray to the Holy Spirit to enlighten you and open your mind and heart to hear the Lord speaking to you through his Word.

Scripture: *Slowly read and reread the scripture passage:*
Now it happened that at this time Caesar Augustus issued a decree that a census should be made of the whole inhabited world. This census—the first— took place while Quirinius was governor of Syria, and everyone went to be registered each to his own town. So Joseph set out from the town of Nazareth in Galilee for Judea, to David's town called Bethlehem, since he was of David's house and line,

in order to be registered together with Mary, his betrothed, who was with child. Now it happened that, while they were there, the time came for her to have her child, and she gave birth to a son, her first born. She wrapped him in swaddling clothes and laid him in a manger because there was no room for them at the inn.

Inspiration Points:

We can re-live this event with the help of our imaginations.

- See Mary and Joseph on their way to Bethlehem; Mary on the donkey, Joseph walking beside her. All her thoughts are on the child in her womb. "The Virgin Mary bore him in her womb with love beyond all telling" (Preface of Christmas)

- After the birth of Jesus: see Mary and Joseph and what they are doing, feel the cold, hear the wind blowing through the open cave. Watch how Joseph does all he can to protect Mary and the child from the cold, gathering hay and sticks for the fire while Mary cuddles her baby and ponders who it is that is in her arms. Be there with them in silent adoration or speak to Mary or Joseph in whatever way comes to you.

• Jesus came to bring us life. "I have come that you may have life" (John10:10). The celebration of his birth is an invitation to allow him give birth to new life in you. Sometimes we don't live fully. Events and relationships in our past or an injustice at work can lead us into self-doubt, fear, or cynicism and prevent us from engaging fully with life.

Thank God for the gift of life and pray that your relationship with the living and risen Jesus will re-kindle your desire to live for God and others. Your prayer might be, "Holy Spirit, Giver of life, breathe this new life within me."

Reflection:

How hidden are the works of God! It was as if God slipped into our world unnoticed, protected by the goodness of Mary and Joseph while the Roman Emperor sought to increase his economic and political control by a census of the population. Through becoming one of us, God is forever committed to our world. God is silently at work within the hearts of those open to welcome the Spirit, as Mary and

Joseph once did. God nudges us gently to do good, placing new desires in our hearts.

Teach me, Lord, to welcome you into my life today through someone I meet or through your Word in the gospel passage. Come, Lord Jesus and open my heart to receive you and to allow you to be born anew into my life.

Petition:

Ask to have a heart-felt knowledge of God who became one of us for you. Ask this so that, knowing him, you may want to love and serve Jesus, our Lord and God, in all you do. Slowly read and reread the scripture passage, pausing where you want.

Playback:

How did it go? What came to you as you prayed? What stays with you? Did anything stir in your heart as you prayed? Would you feel drawn to stay longer or hold on to a phrase?

Scripture: Luke 2:25–32

Suggestions for beginning your time of prayer:

Presence of God:
For a few moments, or even longer, imagine how God sees you. Father, Son, and Holy Spirit each rejoice at your desire to give this time to prayer. Pray to the Holy Spirit to enlighten you and open your mind and heart to hear the Lord speaking to you through his Word.

Scripture: *Slowly read and reread the scripture passage:*
Now in Jerusalem there was a man named Simeon. He was an upright and devout man; he looked forward to the restoration of Israel and the Holy Spirit rested on him. It had been revealed to him by the Holy Spirit that he would not see death until he had set eyes on the Christ of the Lord. Prompted by the Spirit he came to the Temple; and when the parents brought in the child Jesus to do for him what the Law required, he took him into his arms and blessed God; and he said: "Now, Master, you

can let your servant go in peace, just as you promised; because my eyes have seen the salvation which you have prepared for all the nations to see, a light to enlighten the pagans and the glory of your people Israel."

Inspiration Points:

Enter into the minds of Mary and Joseph as they brought Jesus to the temple to consecrate him over to God: with awe and reverence they enter the temple, the sign of God's presence among them. What are their prayers and hopes for the infant Jesus?

- See the old Simeon; years of longing with a faith-filled heart have opened his eyes to recognise in this child the Light of the World. Simeon, along with many other Jews, longed for the promised Messiah, God's anointed one, who was to save his people. They prayed, fasted, and gave alms to the poor hoping to hasten the day of his coming.

- "Prompted by the Spirit . . ." Simeon's way of life has made his own spirit sensitive to the promptings of the Holy Spirit. His eyes are opened to see in the child the one who would be the Light of the World. "Come Holy Spirit and open my heart and mind . . ."

- "He blessed God . . ." To bless God for all gifts received was central to Jewish prayer. Zechariah in the prayer we call the Benedictus prayed: "Blessed be the Lord the God of Israel, he has visited his people and set them free."

- We too can praise and bless God for the gift of a saviour who would be the light of the world. We can ask for the gift of an ever deeper faith to recognise the presence of God in our world and in our own lives.

Reflection:

Listening to the Word of God, pondering it like Mary, and making time for people around us all dispose us to welcoming the Lord in our lives. Simeon, Anna, Zechariah, and Elizabeth and many other faith-filled Jews waited in hope and increased their longing through prayer and perseverance. Their eyes were focused and their ears attuned to welcome the Messiah, God's Anointed One, Jesus the Lord among them.

Advent is a time to watch in prayer and deepen our longing through hidden gestures of love. It is for each of us to ask the Holy Spirit to free us from any ways of thinking, speaking, and acting that could blind us to the presence of God in our midst.

The early Christians prayed "Maranatha, Come Lord Jesus." We too can make this prayer our own, adding our own petitions. "Come Lord Jesus and free me, heal me . . . Come, Lord Jesus, Light of the world, drive out the darkness that leads us astray . . ."

Petition:
Ask to have a heart-felt knowledge of the Lord made flesh for you so that, knowing him, you may want to love and serve Jesus, our Lord and God, in all you do.

Playback:
How did it go? What came to you as you prayed? What stays with you? Did anything stir in your heart as you prayed? Would you feel drawn to stay longer or hold on to a phrase?

Scripture: Mark 13:33–37

Scripture: *Slowly read and reread the scripture passage:*

Jesus said to his disciples: "Be on your guard, stay awake, because you never know when the time will come. It is like a man traveling abroad: he has gone from home, and left his servants in charge, each with his own task; and he has told the doorkeeper to stay awake. So stay awake, because you do not know when the master of the house is coming, evening, midnight, cockcrow, dawn; if he comes unexpectedly, he must not find you asleep. And what I say to you I say to all: Stay awake!"

Reflection:

This gospel lends itself to a different type of prayer from the others. It is more reflective than contemplative. It calls us to examine ourselves and our way of living in the light of Jesus' words: "Stay awake!" These words call to mind a recurring Advent theme.

Jesus is reminding us that we are like servants in the master's household who have been given responsibility while we await the return of the master. It is a call to stay awake and watch for the ways in which the Holy Spirit might be calling us to be fully alive to the risen Lord. The Lord is not only going to come at the end of time, but is ever coming, ever seeking to be part of our lives.

"Stay awake!" Most people's work calls for alertness: the teacher in his class, the bus driver in traffic, the doctor with her patients. Parents, too, have to be wide awake to what is going on in their children's lives. So, too, with us, the followers of Christ. It is easy to be distracted by many things and fall asleep to the presence of God. We get caught up in work, become self preoccupied. Or maybe we slip into sadness or discouragement and become forgetful that the risen Lord is with us and is ever at work on our behalf. Let us then, in this prayer in the company of the Lord who made us and who continues to remake us, ask the guidance of the Holy Spirit to see if there is anything in our lives that prevents us from being fully awake.

- Is there something we need to do to live a more Spirit-led life? Do we need something like more courage or honesty?

- Is there a fear that is paralysing me, a fear that I need to hand over to the Lord?

- Have past injustices caused me to slip into cynicism?

- Am I sluggish in fulfilling my obligations?

- Am I resisting letting the Lord into my life?

- "Be on your guard. Stay awake!"

- Are there compromises in my life? Am I less than honest in my dealings with people? Is there some weakness or habit that lessens my love for spouse, my family or my friends that calls for an extra vigilance?

- Or is it rather my strengths that are the source of temptation? Have I misused my gifts?

A Grace to Ask For

It is for each of us to ask the Holy Spirit to reveal to us what we need to do and to give us the grace to pray to be followers of the Lord who are fully alive and living with the fruits of the Spirit: "What the Spirit brings is very different: love, joy, peace, patience, kindness, goodness, trustfulness, gentleness, and self-control" (Galatians 5:22).

Maybe there is one of these gifts that the Lord wants to give me this Advent? If nothing comes to mind, don't worry, just keep asking the Holy Spirit to reveal to you how you might respond to Jesus' instruction to "Be on your guard and to stay awake."

Conclude your time of prayer by speaking in your own words to Mary, your mother. Ask her to intercede for you to be a faithful disciple of her Son, alive with the joy of the Holy Spirit, with a faith that endures and grows in the midst of difficulties.

Playback:

How did it go? What came to you as you prayed? What stays with you? Did anything stir in your heart as you prayed? Would you feel drawn to stay longer or hold on to a phrase?

Review:

At the end of the retreat, reflect on the three sessions.

- See what worked and what didn't work without being hard on yourself.

- See what you would like to retain from the retreat, in the shape of an image, or phrase, or resolution. Write it down if that helps.

- Ease yourself slowly back into the routine of daily living.